Business Owner's Startup Guide

Parker Press Inc.
Briarcliff Manor, NY 10510

ISBN: 978-1-941760-25-3

For the latest information and updates to this material, check out:
http://www.reallifelegal.com/updates

Business Owner's Startup Guide

Susan G. Parker, Esq.
and Lynne Williams, Esq.

Real Life Legal™

Helpful Guides for Everyday Legal Matters

Parker Press Inc.

Contents

What This Book's About 8

    A Step-by-Step Guide 10

    Do I Need a Lawyer? 12

Formulating a Business Plan 13

    The Elements of a Business Plan 14

    Why You Need a Plan: Planning, Prediction
    and Financing 15

    Short-term or Long-term Plan 15

Naming Your Business 17

    Business Entities and Names Are Matters
    of State Law 19

    Operating Under an Assumed Name 21

    Impact of Federal Law on Business Names 22

    Switching a Business Name 23

Basics on Business Entities 25

    Impact of State Law 26

    Types of Business Entities 27

        Sole Proprietorship 27

        Partnership 27

        Limited Liability Company 28

        Corporations 29

    Deciding on a Business Form 30

Personal Liability and Limited Liability 32

Hiring Employees or Contractors/Freelancers 34

The Business Tax ID Number 35

The Sole Proprietorship 36

Pros and Cons of a Sole Proprietorship 38

Sole Proprietors Should Have Liability Insurance 38

The General Partnership 40

The Partnership Agreement 42

Sweat Equity 44

Partners' Authority 45

Liability of Partners 45

Departure and Admittance of Partners and
Partner Death or Disability 46

Dispute Resolution 47

The Limited Partnership 48

How Does a Limited Partnership Differ from
a General Partnership? 49

Other Partnership Hybrids 50

The C Corporation 51

How Is a Corporation Created? 53

Legal Formalities 54

What Should the Bylaws Contain? 55

Contents

Corporation Taxation 55

Liability and Payment of Corporate Officers
and Managers 56

The S Corporation 59

Qualification as an S Corporation 60

S Corporations and C Corporations 61

S Corporation Downsides 61

The Limited Liability Company 63

Who Runs the LLC? 64

Drafting the Operating Agreement 65

**What Are the Key Differences Between
an S Corporation and an LLC?** 66

Tax Treatment of an S Corporation and an LLC 67

Different Formalities 68

Raising Capital and Transferring Ownership 69

Disadvantages of an LLC for Raising Capital 70

Special-purpose Entities 71

The Nonprofit 72

Tax Exemption 73

Raising Capital for Your Business 76

Financing with Debt 78

Equity Financing 80

Crowdsourced Funding 81

Special Issues 83

    Is Your Enterprise Locally Regulated? 84

    Will You Be Operating Out of State? 85

**Minority- and Women-Owned
Business Certification** 88

    Do You Qualify? 89

    Does the Process Outweigh the Benefits? 90

Concluding Thoughts 91

Online Resources 93

Glossary 94

About the Authors 96

About Real Life Legal™ 97

    Available Titles 97

What This Book's About

The U.S. has historically been a nation of entrepreneurs. For those with the vision and tenacity to give their own businesses a go, many decisions have to be made. Here we cover the basics to get started.

The U.S. has been a welcoming place for those who dare to make their dreams a reality and, for business owners, this is no exception. In today's economic times, entrepreneurship continues to be a path that many take for different reasons:

- There is increasing support for locally owned and buy-local movements.

- Traditional employees who are cast out of corporate America are reconstituted as "contractors" who form their own businesses or consulting firms.

- Younger generations seek a more balanced work/home lifestyle, which can be realized by owning one's own business.

- With the advent of the Internet, home-based work arrangements and off-site workers are increasingly common.

Access to a global economy has made it easier to reach markets. For example, a niche seller of antique writing instruments would likely not be profitable at a brick-and-mortar storefront in a small town. And yet, with an online presence, the seller's wares can be showcased around the world.

Similarly, when it comes to funding, online resources have expanded the reach for capital. While family and friends may still be the best place to start, crowdsourced funding (or crowdfunding) websites have made it easier for startups to raise funds.

Despite all the ways businesses can get funding and grow, the fundamentals of starting with the proper business entity and a solid business plan are essential. It's important to understand how taxes, personal liability and business agreements play a role in forming a new business.

Issues Startups Face All at One Time

- Selecting a business name.
- Creating a business plan.
- Choosing a business entity.
- Obtaining necessary licenses or permissions.
- Securing Tax ID and separate bank accounts.
- Drafting an operating or shareholders agreement.
- Raising money.

A Step-by-Step Guide

Odds are, if you're thinking about starting a business, or have already started one, you've got the confidence to forge a new path. Often the first legal question that business owners must face is what legal form the business should take. If you're wondering what it means to be an S corporation, a C corporation, or an LLC, you've come to the right place.

Decisions regarding your choice of business entity are based on a number of factors including: ease of formation, cost to form, simplicity of operations where you plan to do business and tax consequences. Oftentimes a lawyer's input is needed to make these decisions because there are a lot of things to consider. Here we give you the tools you need to make these decisions. Your business's legal form, along with a business plan and funding, are the highest priorities for business startups.

One of the thrills (and challenges) of a startup is that many decisions often have to be made at once. As you're deciding which business form makes the most sense, you may be fielding resumes for new hires, considering a lease for business space and trying to write a business plan. Whether you've already been running a business, or plan to start from scratch, there is a lot to consider at the same time.

A few years ago, with their young children in school, Jane and Edna began catering luncheons and tea parties for some corporate business meetings in their area. Edna's husband helped land his employer as a starting account, and the business took off. With their children mostly grown now, Edna and Jane want to expand their business and offer large-scale catering. Their plan is to move the operation out of Jane's kitchen and sign a lease for a commercial kitchen so they can properly handle bigger events. Here's what they're grappling with:

- Do they need to form a corporation or LLC to run their business?

- They want to apply for a business loan but would need a business plan as part of the application and don't have time to write one.

- The landlord will give them a lease in their personal names, but they don't want all the personal liability if something goes wrong.

- They've been doing business as "Two Cooks in a Kitchen" but they are not sure if that can be the name of the corporation.

- A friend says they should form their business in Delaware because the laws are better there, but they operate in Virginia. What does that mean?

Here are the types of scenarios that business owners commonly face:

Do I Need a Lawyer?

Many factors go into a decision as to what type of business to form. This book is not a substitute for legal advice if needed along the way. Sometimes it's tempting to use an online service to form an LLC or a corporation, and yet, do you really understand the ramifications of those decisions?

We recommend you consult an attorney if any of the following factors apply:

- You anticipate business losses initially.
- You will have co-owners and:
    - Some owners will work in the business and others won't.
    - Some owners will invest in the business and others won't.
    - Family members will be co-owners.
    - There will be classes of stock or levels of participation in the business.
    - Investors are promised return on investment.
- You will need an operating agreement (LLC) or shareholder's agreement (corporation).
- You're not sure whether startup capital will be a loan (debt) or an investment (equity).
- You aim to take your business public eventually.
- The business will own intellectual property—copyrights, trademarks, or patents—or plans to license any of these.
- You plan to integrate your business planning with your estate planning.
- You hire employees or contractors.
- There is a plan to do business overseas.
- You buy a franchise or an existing business.

Formulating a Business Plan

A business plan is a blueprint that covers the main elements of owning and operating a business. It is a living document that keeps owners focused and is essential if an owner plans to raise capital from outside sources.

In the world of small business, there is a tendency to be informal. And yet, a good business plan can help you keep your focus by mapping out the essential ingredients needed to form and grow your business. If you plan to seek funding from others, it's essential to have a business plan.

A business plan is a good idea whether you start a small consulting business, a professional practice, a retail operation or an import-export business, to name just a few possibilities. A business plan helps you set ideas to paper and think things through.

The Elements of a Business Plan

Your business plan is a roadmap showing where you are, where you want to go and how you will get there. In general, the elements of a business plan include:

- Business overview.
- Industry analysis.
- Description of the likely customer base.
- Competitors, along with their strengths and weaknesses.
- Competitive advantage you may have.
- Operations plan.
- Marketing plan.
- Financing plan.
- Management team.

A business plan is what you'll need to get in the door with lenders, major customers and investors. You'll want to put your best foot forward and show how your team, experience and the research you have done supports the idea that your business will be successful.

Why You Need a Plan: Planning, Prediction and Financing

Your business plan will be useful in a variety of ways:

- It is a device for crystalizing the goals you have set for your business and should be reviewed periodically to see if you are on track.

- It can be used as a planning tool to reveal weaknesses in your business structure, financing or operations.

- It enables you to solicit capital for your business, sharing it with banks as well as potential individual investors.

You can also share the plan with individuals in your line of business and receive expert advice. Some of the people that you should meet with to review your plan include owners of similar businesses (unless they will be direct competitors), business mentors, trusted friends, potential customers, economic development entities in your community and the U.S. Small Business Administration.

Short-term or Long-term Plan

A one-year time frame is best for you to develop short- and long-term objectives with your business plan. Long-range planning is very difficult because the conditions impacting your business can change radically in even a year's time. After a year, you'll want to reassess the business plan and revise as warranted. You'll see whether your goals are realistic, whether economic conditions in your field were as you anticipated, whether your customer base is as predicted and whether your financial predictions were accurate. If all is as predicted in your business plan, bravo! Most likely, however, one or more of your predictions will turn out to be inaccurate, and it will be time to sit down and revise your business plan. By this time you will have more reliable information, and you can produce a business plan with more predictive validity.

Mark developed a business plan for a used bookstore he wished to open, laying out how he would obtain stock and how he would market the store to potential customers. The store took off slowly but became increasingly popular. However, Mark discovered that many of his customers asked him to order new books for them—usually cookbooks and coffee table books. At the end of a year, Mark revised his business plan and decided to create a section of new books in the store while discontinuing the sale of some of the genres of used books that were not popular.

Naming Your Business

Naming your business involves giving thought to your web address, availability of a desired business name and sometimes even whether a proposed name will infringe another's copyright or trademark protection.

Business names have several dimensions. Even before you decide what kind of legal form (e.g., corporation or LLC) your business will take, it's important to think about your business name. You could incorporate with one name, select another name for your web address and operate under a third name for a storefront. You will want to check to see if anyone has a trademark or copyright on the name or names you want to use.

> **Sanford wants to open a spa with the name "Sanford's Spa" in California. While this corporate name is available for use in California, the web name "Sanford's Spa" is not available. There is another spa by that name in Alabama. Sanford decides to stick with the name but selects a different name to be used in his web address. He is not concerned about someone across the country using a similar name for the same business. However, if Sanford's business was selling spa products and his business was largely online, this could present a problem.**

If you're planning to start a local brick-and-mortar service business, you can do a name search at the state level and see if a desired name is available. From there you should consider a website address and whether there are issues with copyright or trademarks. Other things to consider:

- If you're planning to start a business that operates largely online, you'll want a unique identity that isn't confusingly similar to another merchant's name, even if there are no legal issues about the use of the name.

- If your company will do business across state lines, a name used in one state may be confused with a similarly named business operating nearby.

- Don't get so attached to a name that you can't be flexible if someone else is already using it.

Each state has rules on words that cannot be used in a business's legal name. For example, the use of "U.S." or "United States" is often forbidden, as the business may be misunderstood as a government-authorized entity. Often the use of other words, such as *education*, *insurance* or *bank*, is limited to businesses that are properly licensed as educational institutions, insurance companies or banks. These types of businesses are separately licensed and regulated by state law.

Business Entities and Names Are Matters of State Law

Business names are reserved and claimed under state law. Although web names and trademarked/copyrighted names may secure the name for nationwide or worldwide use, the actual legal business entity, such as a corporation, LLC, limited partnership or not-for-profit business is formed at the state level.

Regardless of what business entity you decide upon, be sure to check the availability of the name you want under the appropriate state registry.

Sole proprietorships indicate a person is operating in his or her own name and not in a corporate form. These businesses are generally not required to register at the state level, unlike a corporation, LLC, or partnership. For example, if John Smith opens a bookkeeping service, he may call it John Smith's Bookkeeping Services. If he operates as a sole proprietor, his state may require no state registration. However, if instead John Smith calls the business AAA Bookkeeping Services, that would be operating under an "assumed name" and likely would require some registration at the county or state level.

Each state maintains a system for assigning names to these various types of entities, and you'll want to select a name that is not in use or not confusingly similar to a name already in use. At the state level, here's how that's done:

- Corporate names or names of LLCs are often in searchable online databases at your state's Secretary of State's office, Department of Corporations, or similar type of state agency.

- Partnerships and limited partnerships may be registered at the county or state level; you should check what applies in your state. If a partnership is operating under an "assumed name," i.e., not a person's real name, it would be registered under an assumed name directory at either the county or state level.

- Sole proprietorships (businesses not in corporate form) may not have a registry, but business licenses may still be required. For example, a doctor, lawyer or CPA may operate as sole proprietors, yet the individual would be required to hold a state issued license that he/she is indeed a doctor, lawyer or CPA.

Each state has its own rules to indicate whether a business is a corporation or not. For example, in New York, "Inc.," "Corp.," and "Ltd." indicate that the business is a corporation. "Co." indicates the business is a partnership. The phrase "LLC" indicates the business is a limited liability company, nationwide.

There is no federal registry when it comes to available business names, although certain names may be trademarked.

Since each state has its own registry, the same business name can be legally used in more than one state. If you are in a metropolitan area, which includes several states, like New York, New Jersey and Connecticut, or in the District of Columbia, you may want to select a corporate name that is unique and will not be confused with a similar business licensed in another nearby state.

Sam plans to open an eyeglass store with the name "Sam's Vision Works" in upstate New York near the Massachusetts border. He checks the New York Department of Corporations name registry and discovers he can open his business in that name. He does not realize that just across the border in Massachusetts, an optician is operating under the name "Vision Works Inc.", which is registered as a corporation in Massachusetts. If both merchants draw from the same customer base, it may be confusing to have the same name, and one could lose business to the other, or could benefit! Sam reads some online reviews of "Vision Works Inc." in Massachusetts and discovers they get bad reviews. He decides to change his business name to avoid confusion.

Operating Under an Assumed Name

If a business is operating under a different name than its true legal name, then it is operating under an "assumed name." This can occur whether the true legal name is a corporate name or an individual's name. For example, Bob forms a corporation named "123 Main Street, Inc." which will own his hardware store. The sign on the store says "Hammer and Nail Hardware." Bob is operating under an assumed name.

In most states, if you don't operate your business under its legal name (the name of your LLC or corporation, or your own name if you do not form a legal entity), you must typically file a **"Doing Business As (DBA)"** form with the appropriate governmental agency. Often these forms are filed at the county level, but you can also be required to file them with your state's Secretary of State or department of corporations or similar regulatory agency.

Joe MacHenry has worked as a computer repair person using his own name for many years. Joe decides to lease retail space so he can teach computer classes and have a larger drop-off computer repair service. He plans to call the storefront "Joe Mac's Computer Shack." While it's likely a good idea for Joe to form a corporation or LLC to protect against liability, if he does not, he must still file a DBA in the name of "Joe Mac's Computer Shack." The DBA form will require him to indicate the assumed name, place of operation and contact information for the true owner of the business.

Impact of Federal Law on Business Names

Although business names are selected at the state level, clearance at the state level alone may not be enough. Oftentimes a name may be trademarked, copyrighted, or subject to service mark protection under federal law. So even if you can secure the name for your business under a state database, you may want to check it further to avoid infringing on another's use of the name.

If the name you want is subject to trademark or copyright protection, the owner of that trademark or copyright could sue you for infringement, even if it is legal to form using that name in your state. The simplest way to avoid this problem is to search the U.S. Patent and Trademark Office database to determine if there are any names that could cause confusion with the one you select. A simple Internet search can also reveal if this is a potential problem.

Phil and Barbara started a newsletter business called "Green News You Can Use, Inc." They sold their newsletters to merchants of "green" products. Merchants put their own name on the banner of "Green News You Can Use." Shortly after Phil and Barbara made a huge sale to a major home improvement store, they received a "cease and desist" letter from a national magazine who claimed they owned the copyright to the phrase "news you can use."

Phil and Barbara consulted a lawyer who did not believe the national magazine could win on the copyright claim. Yet if a lawsuit ensued, Phil and Barbara could easily pay $25,000 in legal fees because the national magazine had deep pockets. They decided to select another name for their newsletter to avoid wasting their time and money on a battle that would divert their attention from their business.

In the early stages of your business, it's easy to become stuck on one name that you love. But don't become so committed that you can't change the name if you find it is being used by someone else, the web name is taken, or that you may be infringing on a name already in use. It is not always possible to know in advance if you are infringing on someone else's name. But to the extent you are aware that there could be confusion, it's best to avoid using a confusingly similar name. This is especially true if the name you choose sounds like the name of a national brand.

Switching a Business Name

When it comes to naming a business, sometimes an existing business that switches to another form will want to keep the same name or will choose to operate under an assumed name. Again, it depends on the type of business and what the owner is trying to achieve.

MJ is a dog walker and does business in her own name. Clients pay her personally and she operates as a sole proprietorship. She does not have a separate legal entity for her business. When MJ learns someone has sued a fellow dog walker, she decides to form a corporation to protect against personal liability. MJ forms "MJ Dog Walking, Inc.," as her business. This is not a simple name change. In this example, the business has converted from a sole proprietorship to a corporation.

Each state has a simple procedure for changing business names. For corporations and LLCs and other registered entities, you would typically change the business name by filing a certificate or form that indicates the new name, old name and affirms the contact information. Of course, the new name has to be available under the state registry.

If the only thing that changes is the corporate name, then the tax ID would remain the same. However, bank accounts, merchant accounts, credit cards and similar items must often be modified to reflect the change.

Basics on Business Entities

The most common question people ask when they are starting a business is what type of form it should take. That depends on a number of factors. One size does not fit all.

The most common types of businesses formed are C corporations, S corporations, LLCs, partnerships and sole proprietorships. Some people bandy these terms about when they say they want to form an LLC, a C corporation or an S corporation, though many don't really know why one form should be picked over another.

Each state has its own requirements on how to form LLCs, corporations, limited partnerships, or special-purpose businesses, such as professional practices (doctors and lawyers), banks, insurance companies and educational institutions. There are a number of variables when it comes to deciding which form is best for you. Factors to consider include: personal liability, tax consequences, the ability to raise capital or go public and what would happen if your business went under.

Impact of State Law

It is impossible to outline the variables and details of each state's law when it comes to business entities. Federal tax law is often the superseding concern when it comes to how a business entity will be taxed. But state laws do have an impact and, depending on what issue you might have with your business, these details can be important. For example:

- In New York, holders of 20% or more of a corporation have the right to petition for dissolution if the owners of the rest of the corporation are engaging in questionable conduct.

- In Delaware, it's harder for a personal creditor to get an LLC owner's interest because a charging order is required. This prevents the creditor from attaching a member's interest and forcing dissolution of the LLC.

- Nevada affords greater privacy for owners of corporations.

Certain states are known to have "friendly" laws when it comes to certain things like privacy, creditor rights, taxation or rights when a corporation battles another corporation or even its own shareholders. Most businesses are formed in the state in which they plan to operate, but corporate structures can change and expand as a business grows. Changes are made to take advantage of certain state laws that may be better for a corporation's operations, tax liabilities, environmental regulation or other business issues.

Types of Business Entities

Businesses can be conducted in a variety of ways. Following are the basic business forms that you should consider:

Sole Proprietorship

This business form requires no set up whatsoever. Whether you are a tutor, consultant, or plumber, you operate your business under your own name. There are no forms to file with the state unless you do business under an assumed name or your state requires licensing for your profession.

- Earnings and deductible expenses are reported on a Schedule C filed with your personal tax return.

- There is unlimited personal liability for the owner, but you can purchase liability insurance to cover risk. However, if a lawsuit is filed against you that exceeds your liability coverage, you can be personally liable.

Partnership

This is similar to a sole proprietorship, except there is more than one owner. No formal agreement is required, but it's a good idea to have one. Minimally, the sharing of partnership profits and losses should be covered in an informal agreement.

- Some states require partnerships to be registered.

- Partnership tax return items are reported on a personal return, generally in proportion to an ownership interest.

- There is unlimited personal liability for the partners, and each can be liable for the actions of the others.

- Owners can be individuals or other businesses or legal entities.

A "limited partnership" is a type of partnership entity that permits different classes of partnership ownership interests and ownership rights. It is different than a regular partnership.

Limited Liability Company

This is a separate legal entity that is formed at the state level, has its own tax ID, and is managed by a manager. It is owned by "members" who may be individuals, corporations, trusts or another LLC.

- LLCs are formed in accordance with state law and typically, the phrase "LLC" must appear in the name.

- Articles of organization and an operating agreement set out how the business will run. States may have rules as to what these agreements provide.

- LLCs must have at least one member. If the LLC is a one-member LLC, it may not be required to file a separate tax return. Instead, the single-member LLC may report any earnings/losses as part of the owner's tax return.

- States have "default" rules on how these entities run if there is a non-members' operating agreement.

Corporations

These are separate legal entities that are formed at the state level, usually by filing a certificate of incorporation. These businesses are owned by shareholders and are run by a board of directors. A corporation's bylaws spell out how the corporation will run, and owners may have a shareholders' agreement to spell out rights among one another.

- A C corporation pays taxes at corporate tax rates. After a corporation pays taxes, it may distribute "dividends" to shareholders that are then taxed as income to shareholders. This is why corporations are said to be subject to "double tax."

- An S corporation is a corporation that elects special tax treatment to create tax advantages for the business owners. With an S corporation, the corporation is not taxed at the corporate level, but instead is generally taxed by passing through items of income and loss to an individual owner's return. There is flexibility on allocating distributions and wages. With an S corporation:

    - There must be fewer than 100 shareholders, all of whom must be either U.S. citizens, resident aliens or a certain type of trust. Corporations cannot own shares of an S corporation.

    - There can only be one class of stock, but it can have certain shares as voting and a second tier as non-voting.

- Shareholders pay taxes based on their pro-rata stock ownership.

- Certain types of businesses cannot be S corporations including insurance companies, certain financial institutions, and those that derive a good share of income from Puerto Rico or other U.S. possessions.

Deciding on a Business Form

Business entities differ in ease of formation, protection against personal liability, tax treatment, tax rates, state filing fees, annual state reporting requirements, and what's required to operate the business from a legal standpoint. Often, personal liability (limiting it) and business taxes (how they are treated) drive the selection of business entity. Federal tax law determines the tax treatment of legal entities.

Factors in Choice of Business Form

- Number of owners
- Elimination of personal liability
- Business operating agreement and ease of operation
- State fees form Annual registration fees
- Tax treatment of the business and owners
- Place of formation

When deciding what type of entity to form, an attorney or accountant with knowledge of business formation is your best resource to help you understand tax and other consequences. Some of the variables to consider when you form a business are:

- **Personal Liability of Owners:** Corporations, LLCs and some types of partnerships shield their owners from personal liability. Owners are always personally liable with a sole proprietorship or a general partnership.

- **Types of Ownership:** Corporations with more than one class of stock and limited partnerships enable a business to have owners who run the business and owners who are out of the day-to-day operations. This may be a valuable feature in some types of businesses.

- **Place of Formation:** Some states have more favorable rules than others when it comes to corporations and LLCs. For example, Delaware, Wyoming and Nevada have "corporate-friendly" laws that may benefit your business. However, if you operate your business in another state (not the state where you formed) you will likely have to register as a foreign corporation in the state where you operate.

- **Tax Treatment:** Federal tax laws determine the tax treatment of a business entity. Depending on the form, there may be flexibility as to whether an owner's compensation is subject to social security tax, or whether it is treated as dividend income which is not subject to these taxes.

- **Fees to Form:** State and local fees apply to form and annual register a business. State fees vary by type of entity. If all other factors are equal, the choice of business entity may depend on which form has the lowest state fees.

Generally, to form a corporation or an LLC, the state requires a registration fee. Some states also require that certain businesses publish notice of the formation. Although new business owners may pick one type of business over another to save these initial filing fees, the decision may prove to be short-sighted.

Tom and Eli are mechanics who decide to join forces and open a service station. They had been operating as a partnership but are now considering an LLC or a corporate entity to protect against liability. They plan to purchase certain equipment and fix up a leased space, which will require a considerable investment on their part. They are not sure they will recoup these expenses in the first few years because of these upfront costs.

Based on their own research, they determine they can save annual filing fees if they form an LLC and not a corporation. But after speaking with a lawyer, they learn that although a corporation has higher annual filing fees, by forming an S corporation, they can take advantage of the "pass through" losses and deduct them on their personal tax returns. The value of the losses on their personal tax returns will more than make up for any annual license fees. They determine that forming an S corporation, rather than an LLC, makes more sense in view of their large upfront startup costs.

Often an understanding of the big picture can save costs in the long run.

Personal Liability and Limited Liability

Some business forms, such as LLCs, corporations and limited partnerships, shield owners from personal liability. With a sole proprietorship, or a general partnership, the owners are personally liable for the debts of the business, which includes satisfying a legal judgment against the business. While a business can purchase insurance to cover the risk, this may not be an airtight solution.

Henry runs "Henry's Hairscapes," a sole-proprietorship hair salon in a five-store strip shopping mall. One of Henry's workers left a hair iron turned on and after hours, this led to an explosion that caused great damage to Henry's premises and those of the adjacent businesses. The neighboring storeowners and the landlord filed suit against Henry for over $2 million in damages.

Since Henry operated his business as a sole proprietorship, he is personally liable for all of the debts, losses and judgments against his business. Although Henry had liability insurance for this type of situation, the policy is limited to a $1 million payout. If the neighboring storeowners and the landlord successfully sue Henry for more than $1 million, his personal assets, such as his home or car, could be sold to satisfy the judgment. The fact that Henry's employee was at fault, will not affect Henry's liability to the other storeowners or the landlord.

If Henry's Hairscapes was an LLC or a corporation, Henry would not be personally liable for the business debts or liabilities of the business. Even if lawsuits against the business exceeded Henry's insurance policy, his creditors could not seize his house or car. Only assets in the business name could be sold to satisfy creditors.

While many businesses can purchase a variety of liability or other types of insurance to hedge against risk, only certain types of businesses, such as corporations or LLCs, shield owners from personal liability. Certain types of businesses are at greater risk of being sued, for example:

- Any business owner can be responsible for a slip and fall on business premises.

- Food service businesses can be liable for claims (legitimate or not) of food poisoning or other food-related lawsuits.

- Businesses involving vehicle transportation may be held liable for claims by passengers in the vehicles, but also suits resulting from a business vehicle being involved in an accident.

Many businesses choose to operate as corporations, LLCs, or limited partnerships so that the owners are not personally liable for the debts of the business. For business owners who have substantial personal assets, a separate legal entity should be selected to operate a business.

Hiring Employees or Contractors/Freelancers

Regardless of the type of business entity you form, or if you operate as a sole proprietorship, you can hire employees or contractors to work for you. Payroll taxes and other tax rules will apply once you hire workers and you will be required to file reports with the IRS and your state, as applicable. Also many federal laws, concerning hiring, firing, fair wage/hour laws, pensions, benefits, mandatory leave, disability and other matters may also apply to your business. These laws affecting employer/employee matters are beyond the scope of this book.

The Business Tax ID Number

If the business will be operating under your own name and is not a separate legal entity, use your social security number as its tax ID. The income of the business is reported on a Schedule C and filed with your tax return.

However, if you form a business as a separate legal entity, the business will file its own tax return and you would apply to the IRS for an "Employer Identification Number (EIN)." The EIN, or tax ID, functions like a person's social security number, but for businesses.

You can apply for an EIN directly on the IRS website: https://sa.www4.irs.gov/modiein/individual/index.jsp. Even if you don't intend to have employees for a while, you'll need a tax ID to:

- Open a bank account in the name of the business.

- Ensure tax issues related to your business are separate from your own personal tax matters.

- Report payments to independent contractors or 1099 workers.

- Get credit in the name of your business.

The Sole Proprietorship

The sole proprietorship is the simplest form of business entity, both to create and to manage. It offers no special tax breaks and no protection from personal liability.

In essence, a sole proprietorship is a business entity that is identical to you, the founder. There are usually no papers to file with your state unless you operate the business under an assumed name. For example, if you are a party planner and customers pay with checks made out to you, you are operating a sole proprietorship. If you operate as "Patty's Party Planning" and are not a corporation or LLC, you are operating under an assumed name.

With a sole proprietorship, all profits and losses are reported on your income tax return on a Schedule C. These tax items may provide deductions of losses against other income you report. Depending on the nature of your business, you may be able to deduct a portion of the cost of a home office or the cost of utilizing your personal automobile for business purposes.

It is easy to transform a sole proprietorship into another business entity.

Joyce works part time for an insurance company doing financial analyses of insurance products. She gets no deductions against her W-2 income for her work as an employee. Joyce starts a small bookkeeping business, working out of her home. In the first year of the business, Joyce purchases office supplies and software and attends a professional seminar. All of these costs are deductible against her bookkeeping income as reported on Schedule C of her tax return. In her first year, Joyce has a loss in her bookkeeping business, which can be used to offset some of Joyce's W-2 salaried income.

Pros and Cons of a Sole Proprietorship

The biggest downside of a sole proprietorship is that the owner is personally responsible for the company's debts and liabilities, including any judgments against the company. So, if your business is sued for some sort of injury on your property, or you did something wrong and caused damage to another, you can be personally responsible to satisfy the judgment. Any assets you own in your own name may be available to satisfy a judgment against your business.

Sole proprietorships are good for people who want to have a business on the side. It's often a good option for people who are in transition. If you work in a field where there is little or no risk of a lawsuit that could put your personal assets at risk, this may work fine. However, if you have something to lose, it's essential to have insurance in an unincorporated business.

Sole Proprietors Should Have Liability Insurance

With a sole proprietorship, you want to be sure that there is little risk that you will be sued. And if you are sued, or a claim is made against you, it can be handled with insurance or your own assets.

Terry has a "real" job during the day but started a business on the side as a seamstress. She's altered clothes for years and would like to one day open a custom clothing store. She is an excellent seamstress and has rarely refunded money to an unhappy customer. Terry doesn't have insurance, but has never had a claim against her because of the work she does.

If Terry was doing high-end tailoring on an expensive evening gown or creating custom wedding gowns, she should have an errors and omissions insurance policy in place to protect her in the event someone sues her on a claim that she cannot afford to pay. If Terry regularly worked on expensive clothing, she should consider operating as a corporation or LLC to avoid having any personal liability.

The key to a sole proprietorship is to make sure you have insurance to protect against risk. Otherwise, change to a corporate form or operate as an LLC if you have personal assets you can't afford to lose should something go wrong in your business.

The General Partnership

A partnership is similar to a sole proprietorship except there is more than one owner.

Partnerships are like sole proprietorships in that they are easy to form and operate with little state oversight or fees. However, by definition, partnerships have more than one owner. And owners do not have to be individuals. A trust, another corporation, or an LLC can be a partner in a business partnership.

All states (except Louisiana) have laws that spell out rules on how partnerships run, but oftentimes these rules can be altered if a partnership agreement provides otherwise. Generally:

- One partner can be liable for the acts of the other or others, and there is personal liability for the owners.

- Some states require a partnership operating under an assumed name to be registered or for the existence of a partnership to be indicated by the name, using "and Company" or "and Co." in the name.

- With a partnership, profits and losses typically are allocated among partners in proportion to their ownership interests. However, by agreement and under special tax rules, this can be done differently and special tax benefits can be achieved. This can be important if:

  - There is built-in gain and loss on property contributed to the partnership.

  - Non-recourse debt allocations are important for property contributed to the partnership.

  - There is concern about tax aspects of selling a partner's interest where these factors are important.

- A partnership is taxed as a **"pass through"** entity, which means the partners report items of individual gain and loss on their personal tax returns. A partnership files an information return, but the items are reported on each partner's individual returns.

Partnerships are typically run in accordance with a partnership agreement, which may be merely an understanding among partners or a written agreement. It's best to have documents in writing so there is no doubt as to the agreement if memories fade or circumstances change.

The Partnership Agreement

While your state may not require a written partnership agreement, in the real world you're foolish not to have one. A written agreement lays out the rules of the road and is a point of reference on the main issues that are likely to come up in the business.

It's best to write up a partnership agreement at the beginning when all parties get along. Later, if things go bad and tensions mount, the fair agreement made at the beginning will be a good thing to have.

A partnership agreement defines the rights and responsibilities of each partner. If your agreement doesn't cover all the bases, state law will fill in the blanks.

A partnership agreement typically addresses the following:

- Percentage ownership of each partner.
- Contributions to the partnership, including cash, real estate or services.
- Partners' authority within the partnership and to third parties.

- Who has decision-making authority and over what.
- How new partners can be admitted and old ones retired or terminated.
- How partnership interests can be sold or transferred.
- Whether family members can "inherit" an interest.
- What happens if a partner dies or becomes disabled.
- How disputes will be resolved.
- How partnership distributions will be made.
- Shares of partnership income and loss.

Business Agreements

All businesses that have more than one owner must address management issues, relationships between or among the owners, transfer of interests, voting rights and ownership interests.

- In a partnership, the agreement is a partnership agreement.
- In a corporation, the agreement is a shareholders' agreement and bylaws.
- In an LLC, these subjects are covered in an operating or members agreement.

All agreements concerning how owners will deal with one another and other matters of the business should be in writing.

Sweat Equity

Often in a startup, one person may contribute funds and another owner contributes labor. This is called **"sweat equity,"** and it can take the form of anything from construction, fundraising, research or other work. Often sweat equity gets discounted when another owner kicks in cash. However, you can assign what's known as the "fair market value" of that sweat equity so that the value of the contribution is clear. The fair market value is what the services would have cost on the open market.

By valuing one owner's work, you can determine who owns what, i.e., what each partner's share of the entire enterprise includes. This is important and may affect how much income a partner can draw from the enterprise.

Marcus is a chef who has been asked to be an owner of a restaurant run as a partnership. Though Marcus is a talented chef, he has no funds to contribute. The two other partners agree that while they can contribute financial backing to the partnership, they need Marcus' participation to make the restaurant a success. They agree that because of Marcus' skills as a chef, the recipes that he will bring to the business and the goodwill of his loyal customers, he will receive a one-third share of the business for his sweat equity.

Partners' Authority

Without a specific agreement to the contrary, a partner can commit the partnership (and therefore the individual partners) to a contract, a debt, or other obligation without the other partners' consent. A partnership agreement may change this result among the partners themselves. Within the partnership, it's essential to have a framework for granting authority over certain types of decisions.

A good partnership agreement nails down these rules from the outset. Typically, certain types of decisions (e.g., to expand, buy a business, or close up shop) must be agreed upon by all partners. However, a unanimous vote may not be required for every decision a partnership makes. You want to set out the framework for decisions in writing and decide who will manage the business of the partnership. This is typically done via a managing partner. That person is charged with responsibilities such as accounting, hiring, customer service, negotiating with suppliers and keeping partnership records.

Liability of Partners

Each general partner carries full liability for all the debts of the business, not just for their ownership share in such liability. So a one-third partner is not simply liable for one-third of the debts. A creditor can collect 100% from any owner. This is known as "joint and several" liability. A partner's contribution to the business is at risk, plus each partner is fully liable for all debts, including judgments from lawsuits. Therefore, a creditor can choose to go after one deep-pocketed partner, several or all partners. A partner's liability is not limited to his or her percentage ownership stake in the business.

Ellen, Nancy and Janet form a partnership that delivers gourmet low-calorie meals to subscribers. They each own one-third of the business, and the business is doing well. A bad hurricane hits the area, and the partnership defaults on its deliveries and fails to pay its wholesale suppliers. They are hit with several lawsuits. Ellen is a wealthy woman with many assets. The food vendors sue her, and she is 100% liable. As between Ellen and her partners, she may recover a one-third share from each partner if they have assets. If not, she may be stuck.

The existence of joint and several liability is a serious downside to operating as a partnership, especially if you have personal assets that could be at risk.

Departure and Admittance of Partners and Partner Death or Disability

Businesses are rarely static, and partners may come and go. It's important to develop rules for admitting partners and dealing with partners who want to leave, retire or become disabled. How a person's interest can be bought and paid for must be considered, as well as whether you want a deceased partner's spouse or heirs to continue to own an interest. If not, there must be a mandatory buyout in that type of situation.

There are various ways of dealing with this situation, such as including a clause in the partnership agreement that mandates that any "open" share, such as those due to the departure or demise of a partner, be offered first to the other partners for purchase. This is, however, a complicated topic and, while there is much that business owners can do without attorneys, seeking an attorney's advice on this issue is advised.

Dispute Resolution

A partnership agreement should also include a provision about how it will resolve disagreements. This can include everything from how many partners must vote to agree on something to a mandatory arbitration clause to settle partnership disputes. The last thing anyone wants to sign on for is a costly court battle.

The Limited Partnership

Different classes of partnership interests are permitted in this type of entity. There is flexibility to allocate ownership among those who have a say in the business and those who don't.

One way of limiting the liability of partners and avoiding joint and several liability, is to create a limited partnership. A limited partnership differs from a general partnership in that you can allocate liability and management authority among different tiers or classes of partners: general and limited. Many states require that you file a limited partnership agreement with your state, so you should check with your relevant state agency.

How Does a Limited Partnership Differ from a General Partnership?

Typically, the rights and roles of a limited partner are different than those of a general partner. As a result, a limited partner is only liable for his investment in the business, and is not joint and severally liable for debts or judgments of the partnership.

With a limited liability partnership, a limited partner does not have any management authority. He is actually only an investor in the business. Each limited partnership must have at least one general partner, and that individual or individuals have the authority to manage the business and make legally binding business decisions. It is the limited partnership agreement that lays out which partners have specified responsibilities and authority.

A common phrase that encompasses the role of a limited partner is "silent partner." If someone is interested in investing in your business but doesn't seek management authority, this may be an appropriate entity for your business. A limited partnership is often used for family businesses where some children work in the business and others do not. The children who do not work in the business are given "limited partnership interests," which typically entitle them to a share in the business profits but no say in how the business is run. A general partner, by contrast, gets a share of the profits and has a say in how the partnership is run.

Other Partnership Hybrids

Keeping in mind that a partnership is an arrangement between two or more parties joining together to form a business or run an activity, there can be a number of variables on how these organizations are operated. Following are common types of partnerships:

- **Family Limited Partnership:** These entities may allocate a portion of a partnership business to partners who have more limited interests. Partnership status may be divided into tiers, namely, those who have a say in day-to-day operations and those who are not voting owners but have an interest. This is a common estate-planning entity for a family-owned business in which a business owner seeks to pass the business to all children, some of whom will work in the business and others will not. Special partnership agreements must spell out the particulars of this type of partnership.

- **Publicly Traded Partnership:** These are partnerships that are traded on an established securities market. Essentially, these partnership interests are comparable, economically, to interests in corporations that are publicly traded. These entities are taxed as corporations unless their assets are what are known as "passive," which denotes general dividend, interest, investment or rental income.

- **Limited Liability Partnership:** These types of partnerships are formed under state laws that permit partners (often attorneys, doctors and other professionals) to have limited liability (like a corporation) while having the benefits of a partnership entity. This avoids the need for many of the corporate formalities that would otherwise apply.

The C Corporation

A corporation is a separate legal entity created according to state law, which governs how it operates. Though registered by states, corporations are subject to both federal and state taxes.

A corporation is organized by a "certificate of incorporation" or charter, which brings it into existence. Each state has a body of law that governs how corporations formed in its purview shall be run. A corporation is owned by shareholders and run by a board of directors who may hire officers and employees to run the day-to-day business.

A corporation exists separate from its board, shareholders and employees. It is a separate entity whose life continues beyond the departure of any or all managers, of any or all employees, and shareholders. A corporation need only have one shareholder and has unlimited existence.

Public Versus Closely-held Corporations

- A business like IBM or General Motors is a "publicly held" corporation in that its shares are owned by members of the public.

- A "closely-held" corporation has only a few shareholders, often as specified in a shareholders' agreement.

- Shares of a closely-held corporation often can only be bought and sold by other shareholders. They are not as easily tradable as a publicly held corporation.

How Is a Corporation Created?

A corporation is created under state law, which gives it permission to operate. The state of incorporation determines which laws apply to the corporation. However, a corporation that does business outside of its "home" state may also be subject to laws and requirements in other states or countries as well.

With a sole proprietorship or a partnership, typically you start your business and that's that. With a corporation, you must file the required paperwork in your state, along with a filing fee, which ranges from a low of $50 (in Colorado, Hawaii, Iowa, Mississippi and Oklahoma) to a high of $345 in South Carolina.

The Articles of Incorporation, which are part of the filing, contain basic information about the corporation, including its name and address, how and by whom it will be managed and the number and type of shares that will be issued. Remember, a corporation is not owned by its founders; it is owned by its shareholders.

While there is an abundance of online businesses that will form your corporation or LLC, there is often more to it than just filing. Initial bylaws and other documents must be in place in order for a corporation to be properly set up.

Corporations may also be subject to annual state filing fees. These fees are in addition to taxes, and you should check your state's laws to learn the particulars.

Legal Formalities

As part of the incorporation process, a new business should prepare bylaws, understand the duties and responsibilities of corporate directors (the managers), the owners (the shareholders) and the officers of the Board of Directors. Annual meetings of the directors and the shareholders are required in most states, and those should be scheduled in the bylaws.

Documentation of a corporation's activity is important to have in place. Corporations are required to hold scheduled director and shareholder meetings, prepare and retain minutes from those meetings, adopt bylaws and update them regularly and meticulously record stock transfers. These reporting requirements are more onerous than for an LLC.

Minutes are maintained to record and document the major actions and activities of the corporation. In a one- or two-person-owned corporation, this paperwork may be overlooked, but documentation is important to reflect corporate decisions, especially if there is a dispute among owners.

What Should the Bylaws Contain?

A corporation's bylaws spell out how the business will be run. You want to be sure that you write the rules of the road the way you want them. Bylaws typically cover:

- How shares are issued and paid for.
- The rights and restrictions imposed on shareholders.
- How and when the corporation may make distributions to shareholders.
- How often Board of Directors meetings must be held.
- When shareholder approval is needed to sell assets, merge with another corporation or dissolve.

Typically, each state has a law that outlines a "default" setting in the event that your business did not properly create bylaws or there is a dispute among shareholders about how something is to be done.

Corporation Taxation

A traditional corporation, sometimes referred to as a C, is subject to corporate income tax on its profits. In addition, the shareholders receive distributions known as dividends. Corporations pay corporate tax on profits, and shareholders pay taxes on the dividends they receive, even though a corporation gets no deduction for the dividends it pays. For this reason, it is commonly said that corporations are subject to dual taxation. Corporations are subject to tax on their earnings and shareholders pay income taxes on the earnings paid out by the corporation as dividends.

Corporate earnings and profits are taxed at graduated corporate tax rates of 15% to 35%, and the rates are usually lower than the top income tax rates of an individual business owner. For example, the first $50,000 of a corporation's earnings is taxed at 15%. There can be accumulated-earnings taxes if a corporation doesn't distribute earnings as dividends. These rules are quite technical, and you should consult a qualified accountant or tax attorney to determine whether the tax situation of the corporation will be to your financial benefit or whether it makes sense to form an S corporation.

Liability and Payment of Corporate Officers and Managers

If a corporation is properly formed, its owners have limited liability for actions and activities of the corporation. However, if you run the business and its funds as if they were your own personal bank account, you can run into trouble. When the lines get blurred between your personal activity and the corporation's activities, a court would have the power to look beyond the paperwork in place and "pierce the corporate veil."

"Piercing the corporate veil" involves a court's determination that despite the immunity of shareholders from liability, there is significant evidence that the corporation has not properly kept books and records, maintained filings with the state or properly allocated income, earnings, and profits on the books and accounts of the business. In short, you can't properly set up books and records and divert corporate funds for personal use or commit fraud.

Small corporations and their owners are at risk if they are undercapitalized and the directors and officers co-mingle their personal assets with the corporate assets. Corporate shareholders may be held liable for the debts of, and judgments against, the corporation if this occurs.

Corporate directors may receive per-meeting payments or an annual fee for serving as a director. If a corporation pays the directors for serving on the board, the directors must report the income on their own tax returns, as self-employment income. However, any board member who is also an employee of the corporation gets paid as an employee, with the corporation doing the withholding, reporting and payment of payroll taxes.

Margie, Dan and Alice form a three-person corporation, "Bikes-R-Us," renting bikes out in a resort community. Initially, the shop was small and seasonal. But it has now become very popular, and the owners would like to remain open year-round. Since they need more cash to do so, they approach Annie, Dan's sister, who agrees to invest $25,000 in return for shares in the business. The corporate structure is as follows:

- **The Board of Directors consists of Margie, Dan and Alice as Chair, Secretary and Treasurer, respectively. They are the management team, and they meet each quarter to analyze financial performance and review operations. The directors have one vote apiece.**

- **The executive team, charged with hiring and supervising employees, ordering inventory, marketing the business and the like consists of just Margie and Dan. Alice's involvement is not on a day-to-day basis since she has a full-time job elsewhere.**

- **Corporate net profits are used to buy inventory, pay rent and fund all other costs of doing business.**

- **The two full-time executives, Margie and Dan, each get a corporate salary plus a year-end bonus when profits are good. Alice receives hourly pay for her part-time work on the Board of Directors. All three board members, along with investor Annie, own shares in the business.**

- The company is not yet able to pay dividends, but when it is able to do so, all four of these individuals will receive dividends in proportion to their shareholdings. Even if dividends are never paid, the stock will appreciate if the business is successful, and the owners of the stock will be able to sell the stock either when they choose to move on or when the business is sold. Or, any of them can choose to sell their shares back to the business.

- If the business is sued and a judgment against the business ordered, the corporate officers and investors are not personally liable for the judgment, nor can their personal assets be utilized to satisfy the judgment. However, they are liable up to the amount of their investment in the business.

The S Corporation

This type of corporation enables the pass-through of income and losses to shareholders which often provides a tax advantage to a small business owner.

S corporations are corporations that have different tax treatment than a C corporation and must meet certain rules to get this special tax treatment. Just as individuals file personal tax returns, C corporations pay corporate taxes pursuant to a set of IRS rules. With an S corporation, it works differently.

S corporations pass their corporate income, losses, deductions and credits through to their shareholders for federal tax purposes. This means that there is no "corporate" level tax and instead, shareholders in an S corporation report their share of income and losses on their personal tax returns. Some points to keep in mind:

- Shareholders are taxed at their individual tax rates.

- There is no double taxation on corporate income.

- Shareholders can use S corporation losses to offset items of income on their personal tax returns.

- A corporation must meet certain tax rules to qualify to be an S Corporation.

Qualification as an S Corporation

To request S corporation status, you must file a Form 2553 with the IRS no later than the 15th day of the third month following an organization's date of incorporation. You may also be required to make a similar filing with your state department of taxation. To be eligible to become an S corporation, the IRS requires that:

- There is a maximum of 100 shareholders.

- Only U.S. citizens, resident aliens and certain trusts can be shareholders.

- There is only a single class of stock for the corporation.

- The corporation must be formed by a "natural" person (not a corporation or another entity) who is 18 or older.

The benefits of pass-through taxation are achieved if these requirements are met. For a small business owner, an S corporation often has many of the advantages of a C corporation without the added corporate taxes.

S Corporations and C Corporations

Like a C corporation, an S corporation has an unlimited existence over and above changes in management or even shareholders. However, in an S corporation, a shareholders' agreement typically restricts share transfers. Small business owners generally want to control how the business will run and who will become new owners.

Tax treatment is the key advantage of electing to become an S corporation. For startups, there are typically business losses in the beginning. With an S corporation, these can be used to offset other income on a shareholder's personal income tax returns. The other big tax advantage of an S corporation is flexibility in how distributions to owners are treated. Salary income is subject to social security taxes, but dividend income is not. This can produce tax savings. We recommend you consult a qualified accountant to discuss how an S corporation election can benefit you.

S Corporation Downsides

S corporations are required to hold scheduled director and shareholder meetings, prepare and retain minutes from those meetings, adopt bylaws and update them regularly and meticulously record stock transfers. This is similar to the requirements of a C corporation. However, in addition, there can be tax issues if a shareholder's income is predominantly from distributions and he/she is an employee as well.

Since most shareholders in an S corporation pay tax based on their share of the profits–even if those profits held for future growth are not distributed in a given year–shareholders may be forced to pay taxes on capital gains that they have not received. In short, the cash flow may not match the distributions. Again, a qualified accountant should be able to help you avoid this types of landmine.

The Limited Liability Company

An LLC is a non-corporate business entity which is created under state law and provides for limited liability and simplified tax reporting.

A **"Limited Liability Company (LLC)"** is a popular choice for small business owners because it eliminates personal liability, which is the downside of sole proprietorships and partnerships, and it enables pass-through taxation, which makes accounting easy. An added plus is that an LLC is also fairly easy to form and run.

Like a corporation, an LLC is something that is formed by filing the proper paperwork at the state level. The fees to form an LLC run from a low of $50 to a high of $520, as in the state of Massachusetts. An LLC is formed by filing the appropriate articles of formation with the state. Each state has its own rules about what it takes to form an LLC. States also impose annual filing fees on LLCs. Check your state to see what the annual filing fees are.

Management is vested in "members," and an operating agreement may place management responsibilities on a certain member or class of members. An agreement can also appoint a non-member manager to run an LLC. Like corporations, LLCs are often subject to state laws concerning annual meetings, voting quorums and other operating matters, if not spelled out in an agreement. Generally, rules for maintaining books and records are more relaxed than for a corporation. Members and managers are not liable for debts of an LLC.

Who Runs the LLC?

An LLC is typically either a member-run LLC or a manager-run LLC. If the LLC is a big enterprise, the members (i.e., the owners) may decide to hire a manager (who is not an owner) to run the LLC. In the absence of an operating agreement, most state laws require that the LLC is managed by all members.

With an LLC, each member will have a right to LLC profits, voting rights and LLC assets (if the LLC is liquidated) according to the value of each member's capital contributions to the LLC. Typically, LLC membership interests cannot be transferred nor can new memberships be issued without the consent of all members.

Drafting the Operating Agreement

An operating agreement details how the LLC will run. It covers:

- Duration of the LLC.

- Rights and responsibilities of members.

- Management structure, including the role of a manager.

- Accounting protocols.

- Voting procedures/agreements.

- Capital contributions.

- Addition of new members.

- Indemnification of members.

- Changing members (death, disability, retirement).

- Transfer rights.

It is possible to have a one-member LLC. That simplifies tax reporting because the LLC is not required to file a separate tax return. An operating agreement can be kept simple and expanded if new members join.

What Are the Key Differences Between an S Corporation and an LLC?

For many small businesses, the difference between an S corporation and an LLC may not matter. But they may if you have multiple owners, tax concerns and plans to raise capital.

Tax Treatment of an S Corporation and an LLC

An S corporation is a corporate entity that receives special tax treatment—more like a partnership than a regular corporation. An LLC may elect to be taxed as a partnership or a corporation. Most small businesses will elect to be taxed as a partnership because this avoids a corporate-level tax, and instead, items of income or loss (and credits and other income tax items) pass through directly to the owners' tax returns. A partnership is known as a "pass-through" entity and so is an S corporation.

An LLC can elect this tax treatment and typically does in a small business. Owners of an S corporation or an LLC that elects to be taxed as a partnership are taxed on all of the income, whether or not it is distributed.

The key difference (and possible advantage) of an S corporation over an LLC is on how salary is taxed. An S corporation pays payroll tax on salaries to owners, but it can make distributions in the form of dividends to owners, which aren't subject to payroll tax. They are subject to income tax on the owner's tax return. However, with an LLC, all income passing through to owners is subject to self-employment taxes but not other payroll taxes, such as unemployment or workers compensation insurance. Here are some tax differences between an S corporation and an LLC:

- S corporations are required to make pro-rata distributions of income, but salary can be unequal. LLC owners do not receive a salary, but all income or loss must be reported pro-rata and is subject to self-employment taxes.

- S corporations are required to file a corporate tax return. The corporate tax return reports each owner's allocated share. Tax returns are different for an LLC:

  - With a single-member LLC, all profit or loss is reported on the owner's individual tax return, and the company is not required to file a separate tax return.

- A two-or-more-person LLC must file a partnership return if it elected to be taxed as a partnership. The partnership tax return will allocate the income pro-rata among owners.

- If an LLC elects to be taxed as a corporation, it must file a regular corporation tax return.

• LLCs can allocate profits unevenly if there is an economic reason to do so; this cannot be done with an S corporation.

It's important to consult a qualified accountant to understand how this may impact you and your business.

In most respects, a single-member LLC and an S corporation have simpler taxes than a C corporation. Treatment of distributions as non-taxable for self-employment tax purposes can result in tax savings to owners and is a key difference between an S corporation and an LLC.

Different Formalities

The S corporation limits the members' liability and avoids the C corporation requirement to set up a , file annual business reports, hold shareholder meetings, keep minutes of the meeting and operate under a formal standard of legal compliance. An S corporation is only permitted to have one class of stock, although it can have voting and non-voting shares. An LLC can have different membership classes, as can a C corporation.

S corporations may have a maximum of 100 shareholders—none of whom can be nonresident aliens and any of whom can be individuals, estates or certain trusts. S corporations cannot have corporations as shareholders. This can be limiting! LLC members are not limited in number or in type; and all states permit single member LLCs.

These differences may be more important depending on the growth and plans for either the S corporation or the LLC.

Raising Capital and Transferring Ownership

An S corporation and an LLC are good choices for small businesses that will likely stay small and not seek a lot of capital from outside investors. With an S corporation, whose membership is limited to 100 shareholders and only certain types of shareholders, this structure may not work well for raising capital among a broad base.

If you are considering raising venture capital in the future, the venture capital firms will usually seek a C corporation as the entity for the investment they make. If you want to deduct early losses on a personal return, and wish to eventually operate as a C corporation, it may be easier to start out as an S corporation. While it may be easy to eliminate an S corporation election, keep in mind that there can be complicated tax consequences on this type of conversion. You'll need advance planning and an accountant to sort this out.

Disadvantages of an LLC for Raising Capital

If you plan to raise substantial outside capital or go public, LLCs may not be the business form of choice. There are a few reasons for this:

- LLCs that are taxed as a partnership and owners receive K-1 tax forms. You can be taxed on income even if no actual distribution is made. Investors often don't like K-1s.

- Many venture funds can't invest in pass-through entities because they have tax-exempt partners who cannot receive "active trade or business income."

- LLCs often have provisions in their operating agreements which detail how cash will be distributed to owners. This may impair the ability of the business to reinvest its cash to grow the business.

- Multi-member LLC agreements are more complicated than typical corporate documents, making them cumbersome for investors to parse and accept.

Special-purpose Entities

There are other types of business entities that are created for a particular purpose. These are less commonly known and often permitted under special state laws.

Many everyday business forms, such as banks, insurance companies, land trusts, real estate co-ops, condo organizations and nonprofits are special-purpose organizations. They are formed under separate laws that spell out what it takes to form and run these businesses in order to comply with state laws and/or achieve some tax or business benefit. If you are contemplating some unique type of business entity, you must check your state laws to determine how to properly form and operate.

These may include cooperatives, condominiums, real estate investment trusts and emerging forms of social entrepreneurship. We do not address them here. Non-profits are the most common type of special purpose entities, discussed below.

The Nonprofit

The traditional model for organizations that serve the community in social support, advocacy and activism is the nonprofit. However, as the economy changes, new models of social entrepreneurship are emerging.

The word **"nonprofit"** is a collective name describing organizations, associations, and institutions in the United States that are neither government organizations nor traditional businesses.

Nonprofits are typically formed as corporations, which then elect "nonprofit" status through a state-government agency. Typically, these agencies have paperwork that must be filed to substantiate the nature of the work and why it should be accorded special preference. In its simplest form, you can get together with friends, neighbors, or other like-minded individuals to form a self-help group, whether it's for sharing tools, childcare or cars. This can be an informal nonprofit. A legally incorporated nonprofit requires a Board of Directors.

Tax Exemption

Once a nonprofit organization is formed under state law, it can apply to the IRS to receive "tax-exempt" status. This enables the organization to receive tax-deductible donations and not pay income taxes on funds applied for its tax-exempt purposes. A special application, known as a Form 1023, must be filed with the IRS to receive tax-exempt status for a nonprofit enterprise. You can learn more about the process at: http://www.irs.gov/Charities-&-Non-Profits/Applying-for-Tax-Exempt-Status

A nonprofit that does not file for and receive IRS approval for tax-exempt status under section 501(c)(3) of the federal tax code cannot offer a tax deduction to donors.

Filing for tax-exempt status involves preparing and submitting information to the IRS regarding the nature of your business, records of contributions and expenses and similar information. While attorneys often prepare these applications, it is possible to file for tax-exemption without an attorney. The process may take up to two years, but is worth the effort for nonprofits that want to afford donors the opportunity to make tax-exempt contributions.

Increasingly, local organizations may be able to work with a fiscal sponsor to take advantage of their tax-exempt status for a small administration fee.

Sharon started a small business tutoring immigrants in English, called "Let's Talk." Her services are donated, but she needs to raise money to purchase books and supplies and rent a space to do the tutoring. A donor became aware of Sharon's business and would like to donate $2,500 if she can get a tax deduction for it.

Sharon learns that applying to be tax exempt under Sec. 501(c)(3) of the tax code would be costly since she would need to hire someone to complete the lengthy application and also pay an application fee. However, "Friends of the Library," a local nonprofit that supports the local public library, is supportive of Sharon's business and offers to serve as a fiscal sponsor. In this way, a donor can receive a tax deduction for a contribution to "Friends of the Library," which would pass the contribution along to "Let's Talk" after deducting a small service fee of two percent.

This is a common strategy used by newly formed, small programs, at least until their budget allows them to file for nonprofit status.

All nonprofits that receive tax-exempt status are exempt from federal corporate income tax, and most are exempt from state and local property tax as well as sales tax. They are not, however, exempt from payroll tax and must also pay tax on income derived from activities not related to their mission. It is very important when you file your initial incorporation paperwork to think hard about your written mission statement so that it is inclusive of all of the activities that you are contemplating.

If you do decide to start a nonprofit, it is important to remember that it is a business just like an LLC, S corporation, or partnership. One of the most common mistakes that startup nonprofits make is failing to create a business plan. A nonprofit business plan should include the elements that a for-profit plan includes—an evaluation of competition, funding sources, a needs assessment, services to be offered and potential clients.

There is a move towards creating businesses that represent the founder's vision, and that vision frequently includes sustainability, environmental responsibility and fair treatment of workers.

Raising Capital for Your Business

A big issue business startups face is getting the funds they need to start and run their businesses. Money is raised either by taking out loans or giving away an ownership interest in the business.

One of the key considerations when deciding on your form of business entity is your ability to raise capital. While you may be using your own assets or those of family and friends for your startup funding, it is best to view investment capital as a long-term issue in the context of expanding your business or selling the business.

Debt is money you borrow to grow or run your business. Lenders do not own a stake in your business. They may have collateral in business assets but, once the debt is repaid, they have no interest in your business.

Equity ownership means someone owns both the upside and downside of your business. If the business makes money, those with equity interests make money. If the business loses money, the equity owner's interest is worth less. Equity investors own a stake in your business; lenders do not.

Debt and Equity

- If you borrow money to run your business, you are incurring "debt."
- If investors give you cash for an ownership interest, that is equity financing.
- The ratio of debt to equity financing is an important issue for business owners.
- If a business borrows too heavily, it is said to be heavily leveraged, and that can be problematic.

Financing with Debt

When you borrow money to run your business, this is known as **"debt."** Essentially, you are taking a loan and using borrowed funds. You must pay back the funds per a loan agreement with a bank, finance company or even a personal loan from family or friends. If you take out a loan, you are funding your business with debt.

- Getting a commercial loan from a financial institution will require good credit on your part as well as a convincing business plan that clarifies how the loan will be paid back.

- Larger loans may also require some collateral; you may be asked to put up personal property (such as your home) as collateral. A lender would record the fact that it has extended you credit to make it a secured loan. Personal loans from individuals who know you are typically made based on your relationship with that person. Often there is no collateral and the only documentation is a promissory note for the loan.

While taking on debt can be scary for a small business owner, it has advantages:

- Debt financing allows you to keep complete control of your business.

- Interest payments on loans are tax deductible.

- Debt financing lets you build credit-worthiness for your business.

If you finance your business with debt and pay it back, this can be a benefit for future borrowing, insurance rates and interest charged on accounts with vendors. However, if you are asked to sign a personal guarantee for a loan, be advised that your personal assets may be at risk.

Think Twice Before Making Personal Guarantees

A personal guarantee on a loan is the same thing as obligating yourself to be personally liable for a business debt.

- People form a business as a corporation or LLC to avoid personal liability for the debts of the business. This means that if your business has a debt and can't pay it back, a creditor can only look to your business assets for repayment.

- If you sign a personal guarantee on a loan, lease or manufacturing agreement, it means that you are promising to pay back the loan or meet the obligation personally If your business cannot.

- Your personal assets (your home, car or bank accounts) may be used to satisfy the debt if the business cannot repay that loan.

Equity Financing

If you give someone a piece of your business in exchange for cash or services, you are giving them a share of the "equity" in your business. This is very different than taking a loan. Why? When a person lends your business money and you pay it back, that is the end of the transaction. When a person gets an ownership interest in your business, they share in the upside and downside.

> **Bob has developed a unique app that can identify the sound of bird calls. He's got the technical know-how to create the product but needs funding to hire help and market the product. He wants to raise $100,000 to get the help he needs. If he borrows $100,000 from his parents and their friends, he will pay back interest on the loan. When the $100,000 loan is paid back, Bob will still own 100% of the company.**

> **If Bob gives his parents and their friends a 30% interest in the company for their $100,000 investment, his company will keep the money no matter what. There is no requirement to repay it. Bob will own a 70% interest in the company. When the company begins making money, the investors will get 30% of the upside.**

The downside of equity financing is that you give up some control of your business. However, if you get the right investor, such as a savvy businessperson, it can be an asset to your business. The important things to consider with equity financing are:

- How you and the investor interact.

- The trust between the two of you.

- Whether the investor brings other benefits to the business.

Equity financing is an alternative to debt financing and often, both debt and equity are used to run a business. With the right ratio of debt and equity, the burden of large monthly loan payments can be minimized and you can keep control of the business.

Crowdsourced Funding

"Crowdfunding" is a way of raising money online through Internet websites such as Fundable, Kickstarter and Indiegogo. Many of the intricacies of what is called "general solicitation" of funds are beyond this book, as are the security-law implications of this type of fundraising for a startup. Here's a taste of how it generally works:

Crowdfunding takes place on an online platform, where a startup or a business seeking to expand turns to a "crowd" of potential backers for money. While these funders usually receive incentives such as free tickets to performances, copies of a book when it's published or gift certificates for meals at a new restaurant, they are not investors in the business. That would be considered a "public offering" and is strictly regulated by the Securities and Exchange Commission (SEC).

While Congress has asked the SEC to issue rules covering crowdfunding, they have yet to do so. However, at least 13 individual states, such as Michigan, Wisconsin, Indiana, Kansas, Georgia and Texas, among others, have been filling in the gap by passing state statutes that permit limited equity crowdfunding of in-state businesses by in-state residents. Check with your own state's office of corporations or of financial regulation to see if your state has passed such a statute.

If there is no state law regulating crowdfunding, you will only be legally permitted to use it for non-equity fundraising. You cannot sell interest in your company through crowdfunding. Most sites that manage crowdfunding allow you to solicit donations to your business and distribute thank-you rewards or premiums for various levels of donations that can range from simple acknowledgments to samples of the enterprise's goods or services and one-time offers.

Special Issues

Local regulation and licensing requirements should be considered for all businesses. There may be state, county, town, village or other local rules that impact your business and require compliance.

Is Your Enterprise Locally Regulated?

Increasingly, the form of businesses are changing and so, too, are the laws that regulate them. Consider Airbnb, which enables those with an account to "sublet" their homes to out-of-town visitors. It may be a great opportunity for the owners to get some extra income and their tourists/tenants to get a good deal, but there are legal issues with sublets. As a result, hotels, condo and co-op boards and others are taking a hard look at the laws. They want to protect their own interests by limiting these short-term sublets.

Here are a few ways that your business may be locally regulated.

- Home occupations: More and more municipalities are regulating the type of businesses you can run from your home.
    - Often regulation occurs through a town or city's land use ordinance.
    - These ordinances often regulate how many non-family member employees may work at the business, how many non-family-owned vehicles may park on the property, and the type of business that may be conducted on the property.
    - Condo or coop boards may restrict business use of a home.
- Types of Businesses/Zoning: Certain businesses are regulated insofar as where they can be located and how they may be run. These can include:
    - Food and hospitality industry, especially those that feature live music.
    - Businesses that involve dangerous products, such as propane.
    - Kennels, which may involve excessive noise.
    - Group homes for the handicapped, disabled and recovering addicts.
    - Liquor stores.

Be sure to check with state and local authorities to see whether the type of business you own may be subject to regulation. Certain businesses, like a microbrewery, may also need permits from the Alcohol and Tobacco Tax and Trade Bureau prior to applying for state or local permits.

Will You Be Operating Out of State?

If you are a business owner who intends to operate your business in more than one state, you will have to consider the laws of other states where you do business, maintain facilities, or undertake sales. Your "home" state is the state where your business is incorporated or where your LLC was formed.

If you operate in other places, you will need to register or "qualify" in those states or countries as well. For example, if you formed your LLC in Delaware but have your physical location in New Jersey, you will need to register as a "foreign" corporation in New Jersey. To qualify to do business in another state, you generally must file a certificate and pay a fee to do business in that state.

Business in Several States

There can be state laws and tax consequences in another state if you:

- Have a physical presence, such as an office or factory, in the state.
- Derive significant income from customers in the state.
- Have employees in the state.
- Pay state payroll tax in that state.
- Have a business license in the state.

Small businesses typically incorporate in their home states. However, depending on the nature of your business, factors such as privacy, liability and minimal corporate oversight may make it more desirable to form in another state (such as Delaware or Nevada) even if your main operations will be in your home state.

Given the paperwork and fees, possibly increased taxes and multiple regulatory schemes, it is advisable to file for foreign qualification only where necessary. That said, each state has its own rules and consequences for failing to register as a foreign corporation. Often if you fail to register, and should have registered, you will owe back taxes and be denied the opportunity to sue someone in that state's courts or respond to a lawsuit against you.

Earning money in multiple states does not necessarily mean that you are doing business in those states.

Brad lives in Boston, and Ron, his business partner lives in Chicago. They incorporated their consulting company in Massachusetts. The bulk of their clients are from Illinois, and Ron is meeting regularly with these clients. The consulting firm may need to file for foreign qualification in Illinois.

However, if they work with clients throughout the country and have occasional meetings with these out-of-state clients in their own home states, they may not need to file for foreign qualification. Earning fees from out-of-state clients does not necessarily mean that you are "transacting business" in those other states.

Minority- and Women-Owned Business Certification

Government and corporate national certification programs are designed to provide resources to minority- and women-owned businesses and other entrepreneurs, and provide an advantage on certain contract bidding.

Special certifications for new entrepreneurs, minority business owners and women may be important for access to funds, business insights and resources these groups provide. The three most prevalent programs are the Minority Business Enterprise (MBE), the Woman Business Enterprise (WBE) and Small Business Administration 8(a) certifications.

Do You Qualify?

To be eligible for the MBE national certification, a business can be located in any state in the United States and must be at least 51% minority-owned. This is a private-sector certification program which assists MBEs in accessing local, regional and national corporate set-aside contracts (contracts that are purposefully set aside for MBEs).

WBEs are similar to MBEs in that the business can be located in any state and must be at least 51% women-owned. Again, this private sector program helps WBEs access local, regional and national set-aside contracts.

The Small Business Administration 8(a) certification, or SBA 8(a), operates differently than the WBE and MBE programs. It is a nine-year business development plan designed to assist minority-owned, socially and economically disadvantaged businesses in any state. This is more of a support and training program in that it not only provides the business access to local, regional and national set-aside federal (rather than private sector) contracts, but also trains the business employees about how to bid on federal contracts. The program also provides the business with mentors and helps create opportunities for the business to enter into a joint venture with a larger business.

Does the Process Outweigh the Benefits?

The paperwork for the MBE and WBE certifications is manageable. However, the SBA 8(a) paperwork and documentation does take a significant amount of time and thought to justify admission into the program. Applicants must show that they are not only a minority-owned business but are also socially and economically disadvantaged and it is not necessarily easy to gather the data to support that argument.

There is also a sense among some potential MBEs and WBEs that carrying such a designation somehow makes them appear less competent than a traditionally owned business or that their professional community considers them to be the recipients of favoritism. Yet others in the community consider it a plus to highlight minorities and women who have achieved a level of professionalism commensurate with the requirements of their businesses.

As an entrepreneur you will have to weigh the plusses and minuses of these three programs and decide whether the benefits outweigh the costs, whether the contract possibilities and connections outweigh the paperwork burdens and the possible reputation negatives. It should be noted, however, that when a new business is created, there is a steep climb to profitability, and the contract set-asides, mentoring and networking that these programs would permit you to access may suggest that they are worth your participation if your business qualifies.

Concluding Thoughts

Taking the time to select the right type of business entity for your needs can be one of the most important decisions you make, even if the journey takes you in new directions.

Being an entrepreneur is an adventure and, as many better-known business owners will tell you, what they planned is not what happened. As you begin this journey of discovery and creation, having the right business entity in place and a workable business plan will go a long way.

We've highlighted the big minefields that entrepreneurs face at the start and offer additional resources in the pages that follow to help you find more information when the time comes. Having your own small business is a rewarding enterprise, so believe that it is worth the effort. It may take longer than you think, but persistence pays.

Online Resources

Resources for Business Startups	
Organization	**Website or Phone Number**
Benefit Corporations	http://benefitcorp.net/
State Labor Offices	http://www.dol.gov/whd/contacts/state_of.htm
Fundable	http://www.fundable.com
Kickstarter	http://www.kickstarter.com
Indiegogo	http://www.indiegogo.com
Tax Information for Businesses	http://www.irs.gov/businesses
Minority-Owned Businesses	https://www.sba.gov/content/minority-owned-businesses
Social Security Administration	http://www.ssa.gov
Small Business Administration	http://www.sba.gov
SBA 8(a) Business Development Program	https://www.sba.gov/category/navigation-structure/8a-business-development-program
Women Owned Small Business (WOSB) Program Certification	https://www.sba.gov/content/women-owned-small-business-wosb-program-certification

Glossary

Bylaws: Document which governs the internal rules on how a corporation will be run and managed by officers, shareholders and directors.

Charter: Usually called the Articles of Incorporation, a corporate charter includes the rules governing the management of a corporation and is filed with a state or other regulatory agency.

Crowdfunding: The practice of funding a business or project by raising contributions, large and small, from a large number of people, usually over the Internet at various crowdfunding sites.

Debt: In the context of a business, debt has multiple meanings. The most common is the amount due to creditors for services and products. Used in the phrase "debt equity," the term debt refers to the equity that an individual has in a business if she loaned money to the business and, when the loan is paid off, the individual no longer has an interest in the business.

Dividends: A payment made by a corporation to the shareholders as a distribution of profits.

Doing Business As (DBA): If a business name is different than the owner's personal name or the entity's legal name, that business will likely have to file a form with either the state or county to register that it is operating under an assumed name.

Employer Identification Number (EIN): An identifying number, similar to a social security number, that is given to a business by the Internal Revenue Service. All tax paperwork includes the EIN rather than the owner's social security number.

LLC: Type of business entity that is formed at the state level and owned by members. May be one member and taxed as a pass-through entity.

Glossary

Limited partnership: Type of partnership with different classes or types of ownership that can provide limited liability for some owners.

Nonprofit: Also called a not-for-profit, this is an organization that uses its revenues to achieve its tax-exempt purposes. It does not make dividend distributions to shareholders.

Operating agreement: Document that governs the management of an LLC.

S Corporation: Regular corporation which meets certain IRS requirements and elects to be taxed as a pass-through entity.

Silent partner: An individual whose involvement in a partnership or LLC is limited to providing capital to the business. A silent partner is also known as a limited partner. (See Limited Partnership, above).

Sweat equity: The ownership interest that is created as a direct result of an individual's labor put toward property upkeep or restoration.

Shareholders agreement: Governs the relationships among owners of a corporation.

About the Authors

Lynne Williams, Esq.

Lynne Williams is a special education attorney who represents families of special needs children at mediation, due process hearings and court proceedings. Lynne has a Ph.D. in social psychology from the University of Southern California and earned her law degree at Golden Gate University School of Law. Ms. Williams practices law in Maine and is a former Special Education Hearing Officer for the state of Maine.

Susan G. Parker, Esq.

Susan G. Parker maintains a law practice in Westchester County, New York, which specializes in estate planning, probate and tax and business planning/agreements. Ms. Parker graduated with a B.A. in history from the University of Pennsylvania and received her J.D. from St. John's University School of Law. She has a postgraduate law degree in taxation (LL.M.) from New York University School of Law.

Ms. Parker is licensed to practice law in New York and Florida, and the U.S. District Courts for the Eastern and Southern Districts of New York, as well as the U.S. Tax Court. Ms. Parker has written extensively on tax and legal subjects for legal publishers and financial firms for almost 30 years. Her first book, *Your Will and Estate Planning*, was published by Houghton Mifflin in 1989.

About Real Life Legal™

Parker Press Inc., the publisher of Real Life Legal™, creates plain-language consumer information on legal, tax, business and financial subjects. Taking aim at information overload and legalese, Parker Press Inc. launched Real Life Legal™ in 2014. Real Life Legal™ provides practical advice, written by lawyers, to help people understand how the law works. Our goal is to provide solid, easy-to-understand information so *you* can decide whether it makes sense to hire a lawyer. Real Life Legal™ wants you to be prepared.

Available Titles

Bankruptcy Basics: Chapter 7 and Chapter 13
Marina Ricci, Esq.

Business Owners Startup Guide
Susan G. Parker, Esq. and Lynne Williams, Esq.

Elder Law: Legal Planning for Seniors
Maria B. Whealan, Esq. and Susan G. Parker, Esq.

Employee's Guide to Discrimination and Termination
Joanne Dekker, Esq.

Estate Planning: A Road Map for Beginners
Susan G. Parker, Esq. and Maria B. Whealan, Esq.

Filing a Homeowner's Claim: Natural Disaster or Not
Dawn Snyder, Esq.

A Lawyer's Guide to Home Renovations
John A. Goodman, Esq.

Available Titles (Continued)

Planning for Pets: Trusts, Leash Laws and More
Joanne Dekker, Esq.

Planning for Your Special Needs Child
Amy Newman, Esq.

Special Needs Education: Navigating for Your Child
Lynne Williams, Esq.

U.S. Veterans: Your Rights and Benefits
Maria B. Whealan, Esq.
with Paul M. Goodson, Esq.

What to Do When Someone Dies
Susan G. Parker, Esq.

You've Been Arrested: Now What?
Maryam Jahedi, Esq.

Notes

Notes

Notes